Watching Nature

Watching the Moon

By Edana Eckart

SCHOLASTIC INC.

New York Toronto London Auckland Sydney
Mexico City New Delhi Hong Kong Buenos Aires

Contributing Editors: Shira Laskin and Jennifer Silate
Book Design: Michelle Innes

ISBN 0-516-25229-1

12 11 10 9 8 7 6 5 4 3   5 6 7 8 9 10/0

Printed in the U.S.A.   61

First Scholastic printing, April 2005

Contents

The Moon is in the sky.

You can see it at night.

The Moon has holes in it called **craters**.

The Moon is a big circle tonight.

This is called a **full Moon**.

The Moon moves around Earth.

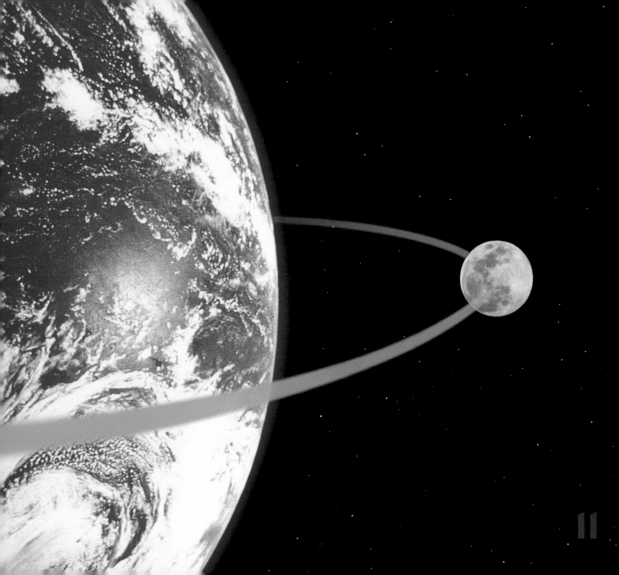

The Moon looks different at different times.

The Moon looks bigger when it is closer to Earth.

Sometimes, the Moon can look very small.

This is called a **crescent Moon**.

Sometimes you can only see **half** of the Moon.

This is called a half Moon.

Some nights, the Moon looks like it is not there at all.

This is called a **new Moon**.

The Moon makes the night sky beautiful.

New Words

craters (**kray**-turz) large holes in the ground
    caused by something such as a bomb or other
    falling objects

crescent Moon (**kress**-uhnt **moon**) the phase
    of the Moon when it is a small, curved shape

full Moon (**ful moon**) the phase of the Moon when
    the side turned toward Earth is entirely lit

half (**haf**) one of two equal parts of something

new Moon (**noo moon**) the phase of the Moon
    when the side turned toward Earth is
    entirely dark

To Find Out More

Books
So That's How the Moon Changes Shape!
by Allan Fowler
Scholastic Library Publishing

The Moon Book
by Gail Gibbons
Holiday House

Web Site
Nova: To the Moon
http://www.pbs.org/wgbh/nova/tothemoon/
Read many interesting things about the Moon and
people who have gone there on this Web site.

Index

About the Author
Edana Eckart has written several children's books. She enjoys bike riding with her family.

Reading Consultants
Kris Flynn, Coordinator, Small School District Literacy, The San Diego County Office of Education

Shelly Forys, Certified Reading Recovery Specialist, W.J. Zahnow Elementary School, Waterloo, IL

Paulette Mansell, Certified Reading Recovery Specialist, and Early Literacy Consultant, TX